The Genesee Diary is far and away one of the most rewarding books I have read in years, because it so beautifully lifts the heart and mind to God and the Saviour.

—*Christianity Today*

I think most readers will find this book [*Reaching Out*] insightful and meaningful as they also reach out. It is a work which can be read and re-read throughout one's life, for at no time do we cease to reach out.

—*Spiritual Life*

I would highly recommend this book [*The Wounded Healer*] to all priests, sisters, and brothers as well as to all who recognize that in calling themselves Christian they are called to be ministers of healing.

—*Review of Religious*

This little book [*Creative Ministry*] is a big step in several important directions. It offers fresh insights and inspiration to anyone engaged in the Christian ministry.

—*Commonweal*

This remarkable book [*Aging: The Fulfillment of Life*]. . . . offers many subjects for meditation, for the benefit of our spiritual life. It will be a source of joy to many people.

—*Spiritual Life*

Other books by Henri J. M. Nouwen

AGING: THE FULFILLMENT OF LIFE

CREATIVE MINISTRY

THE GENESEE DIARY: REPORT FROM A TRAPPIST MONASTERY

INTIMACY: PASTORAL PSYCHOLOGICAL ESSAYS

THE LIVING REMINDER: PRAYER AND SERVICE IN MEMORY OF
JESUS CHRIST

OUT OF SOLITUDE

PRAY TO LIVE: THOMAS MERTON A CONTEMPLATIVE CRITIC

REACHING OUT: THREE MOVEMENTS OF THE SPIRITUAL LIFE

WITH OPEN HANDS

THE WOUNDED HEALER: MINISTRY IN CONTEMPORARY SOCIETY

CLOWNING IN ROME

HENRI J. M. NOUWEN

Clowning in Rome

Reflections on Solitude, Celibacy,
Prayer, and Contemplation

IMAGE BOOKS

A DIVISION OF DOUBLEDAY & COMPANY, INC.

GARDEN CITY, NEW YORK

Library of Congress Cataloging in Publication Data

Nouwen, Henri J M
   Clowning in Rome.

   1. Spiritual life—Catholic authors—Addresses,
essays, lectures.   2. Monastic and religious life—
Addresses, essays, lectures.   I. Title.
BX2350.2.N67   248'.89

Library of Congress Catalog Card Number 78–22423
ISBN: 0-385-15129-2

"Solitude and Community" first appeared in the No. 48, 1978 issue of *UISG Bulletin*, Copyright © 1978 by International Union of Superiors General.

"Celibacy and the Holy" first appeared under the title "Celibacy" in the Winter 1978, Vol. 27, No. 2 issue of *Pastoral Psychology*, Copyright © 1978 by Human Sciences Press.

"Prayer and Thought" first appeared under the title "Unceasing Prayer" in the July 29–August 5, 1978, issue of *America*, Copyright © 1978 by America Press.

"Contemplation and Ministry" first appeared in the June 1978 issue of *Sojourners*, Copyright © 1978 by People's Christian Coalition.

Acknowledgments

This book has its origin in four lectures given to the English-speaking community in Rome.

First of all, I want to thank Harold Darcy for inviting me to spend a semester at the North American College in Rome and for offering me the opportunity to present the lectures on celibacy and contemplation. I am also grateful to Peter Slocombe for asking me to share some reflections on prayer with the students of the Beda College and to Josephine Rucker for convincing me to speak about solitude to the members of the Unione Internazionale Superiore Generali.

I owe a special word of appreciation to Enrico Garzilli and Matthew Clark for their supportive criticisms, to Stephen Leahy and Phil Zaeder for their stylistic corrections, and to Ida Bertoni, Paul Holmes, and David Lancaster for their secretarial assistance.

I want also to express my sincere thanks to Fred Hofheinz and the staff of the Lilly Endowment for creating the possibility of spending time away from "home."

A final word of thanks goes to my friend John Mogabgab, who—as in my other writing—has given his invaluable assistance and support.

to the memory of a very humble man
Pope Paul VI

Contents

Introduction

On the periphery of the circus

This small book was born in Rome. I had always wondered what it would be like to live in Rome for more than a
few weeks of vacation. When the staff of the North American College invited me to join them for five months, I had a
chance to find out.

It took a while to get used to living in a building
overlooking the Vatican as well as the monument of Victor
Emmanuel; it took a while to become familiar with both the
solemnity of the papal ceremonies in St. Peter's and the fervor of the demonstrations in Piazza Venezia; it took a while
to feel at home in a city in which piety and violence rival
each other in their intensity; and it took a while to take for
granted that the devout worshipers in Piazza San Pietro are
as much a part of Roman life as the bohemians on Piazza
Navona. But after a month, the imposing buildings, the
large crowds, and the sensational events seemed little more
than the milieu for something much less visible but much
more penetrating.

During these five months in Rome it wasn't the red car-
dinals or the Red Brigade who had the most impact on me,
but the little things that took place between the great
scenes. I met a few students of the San Egidio community

"wasting" their time with grade-school dropouts and the elderly. I met a Medical Mission sister dedicating all her time to two old women who had become helpless and isolated in their upstairs rooms in Trastevere. I met young men and women picking up the drunks from the streets during the night and giving them a bed and some food. I met a priest forming communities for the handicapped. I met a monk who with three young Americans had started a contemplative community in one of Rome's suburbs. I met a woman so immersed in the divine mysteries that her face radiated God's love. I met many holy men and women offering their lives to others with a disarming generosity. And slowly, I started to realize that in the great circus of Rome, full of lion-tamers and trapeze artists whose dazzling feats claim our attention, the real and true story was told by the clowns.

Clowns are not in the center of the events. They appear between the great acts, fumble and fall, and make us smile again after the tensions created by the heroes we came to admire. The clowns don't have it together, they do not succeed in what they try, they are awkward, out of balance, and left-handed, but . . . they are on our side. We respond to them not with admiration but with sympathy, not with amazement but with understanding, not with tension but with a smile. Of the virtuosi we say, "How can they do it?" Of the clowns we say, "They are like us." The clowns remind us with a tear and a smile that we share the same human weaknesses. Thus it is not surprising that pastoral psychologists such as Heije Faber in Holland and Seward Hiltner in the United States have found in the clown a powerful image to help us understand the role of the minister in contemporary society.

The longer I was in Rome, the more I enjoyed the clowns, those peripheral people who by their humble, saintly lives evoke a smile and awaken hope, even in a city terrorized by kidnaping and street violence. It is false to think that the Church in Rome is nothing more than an unimaginative bureaucracy, nothing less than a rigid bulwark of conservatism, or nothing other than a splendid museum of renaissance art. There are too many clowns in Rome, both inside and outside the Vatican, who contradict such ideas. I even came to feel that behind the black, purple, and red in the Roman churches and behind the suits and ties in the Roman offices there is enough clownishness left not to give up hope.

It is this hope that underlies the four chapters of this book. They were written as lectures for English-speaking sisters, priests, and seminarians in Rome, and they call attention to four clownlike elements in the spiritual life: solitude, celibacy, prayer, and contemplation. My growing love for the clowns in Rome made me desire to clown around a little myself and to speak about such foolish things as being alone, treasuring emptiness, standing naked before God, and simply seeing things for what they are. I came to feel that in this full, imposing, venerable, and busy city there must be a very deep desire to live out the other side of our being, the side that wants to play, dance, smile, and do many other useless things.

Sisters busy with many administrative responsibilities wanted to know about solitude. Seminarians already sensing the dangers of a lonely existence wondered about celibacy as a way of life. Priests aware of the heavy demands of the ministry questioned the possibility of a prayerful life. And everyone going to class at one or another of the Roman universities and becoming more and more involved in the political, social, and cultural life of the city doubted if they would ever be able to satisfy their contemplative needs.

I have called this book *Clowning in Rome* because all the subjects I was asked to talk about seemed to belong to the periphery of the world with which *Il Messaggero* and *Il Corriere della Sera* fill their pages, while at the same time they are central to the life of the Spirit. The four chapters do not follow each other in a logical order. They can be read independently of each other. What binds them together is that they were inspired by Rome and written for sisters, priests, and seminarians living there. I have therefore resisted the temptation to change the speaking style into an essay style or to adapt the text for a general readership. The specific place and audience are too integral a part of these presentations to be taken out. This might give the book a somewhat bumpy character. But when clowning in Rome becomes a smooth performance, there won't be much left to evoke a smile.

CHAPTER I

Solitude and Community

INTRODUCTION

When we reflect on the main events of the past weeks, we come to realize that our world has entered into a state of emergency. In Rome a judge was killed, and Aldo Moro, the leader of the Democrazia Cristiana kidnaped, while five of his bodyguards were assassinated. In Turin a police officer was shot to death, and in Milan two young leftist students were murdered. In Holland, Moluccan terrorists seized a government building and held the country in fear for many hours. In Israel, Palestinian guerrillas killed thirty-four bus passengers, and in Lebanon, hundreds of men, women, and children lost their lives in reprisal actions. In Rhodesia, Ethiopia, and Somalia, a state of war continues after many negotiations. In the United States and many other countries, strikes threaten the economy and reveal deep discontent about living conditions among millions of people. In Belgrade, a world conference on human rights failed to come to any significant agreements, while more violations are reported from the Soviet Union, Argentina, Paraguay, and other countries. The relationships among the main powers of the world are deteriorating, while the chances for a universal holocaust are increasing with the buildup of nuclear arsenals. And so, as we approach the end of the second millennium of the Christian era, our world is clouded with an all-pervading fear, a growing sense of despair, and the paralyzing awareness that indeed humanity has come to the verge of suicide. We no longer have to ask ourselves if we are approaching a state of emergency. We are in the midst of it, right here and now.

You do not have to be a great prophet to say that coming decades will most likely see not only more wars, more hunger, and more oppression, but also desperate attempts to escape them all. We have to be prepared for a period in which suicide will be as widespread as drugs are now, in which new types of flagellants will roam the country frightening the people with the announcement of the end of all things, and in which many new exotic cults with intricate rituals will try to ward off a final catastrophe. We have to be prepared for an outburst of new religious movements using Christ's name for the most un-Christian practices. In short, we have to be prepared to live in a world in which fear, suspicion, mutual distrust, hatred, physical and mental torture, and an increasing confusion will darken the hearts of millions of people.

It is in the midst of this dark world that the Christian community is being tested. Can we be light, salt, and leaven to our brothers and sisters in the human family? Can we offer hope, courage and confidence to the people of this era? Can we break through the paralyzing fear by making those who watch us exclaim, "See how they love each other, how they serve their neighbor, and how they pray to their

Lord"? Or do we have to confess that at this juncture of history we just do not have the needed strength or the generosity and that our Christian communities are little more than sodalities of well-intentioned people supporting each other in their individual interests?

When you asked me to reflect on solitude in the life of the religious community, I realized that I could only speak about solitude in the context of these urgent questions. It would be easy, and therefore tempting, simply to speak about the relationship between solitude and community in general, but it would not be a challenge to you. Therefore, I will try to explain how the emergency situation of the world in which we live can open us to a new understanding of the indispensability of solitude in the life of the Christian community.

I hope to discuss the life of the Christian community under three headings—intimacy, ministry, and prayer—because intimacy ("see how they love one another"), ministry ("see how they serve each other"), and prayer ("see how they pray to their God") are the life-giving forces of a witnessing community. I hope to show how these three aspects of the communal witness are connected with chastity, obedience, and poverty and require a deep commitment to solitude.

SOLITUDE AND INTIMACY

The forces of fear and anger

How can solitude deepen our communal witness to love?
In our emergency-oriented world, fear and anger have become powerful forces in human behavior. Not only do we
see in the daily newspapers how people are driven together
by fear or bound together by anger, but we also start realizing that many religious communities are plagued by a restlessness tainted by fear and anger. We see a growing need
in many religious communities for a place that offers a sense
of belonging, a place where frustrations can be expressed,
disappointments shared, and pains healed. Many religious
communities who in the past felt quite secure and self-
confident, suffer from self-doubt and, at times, from a deep
sense of powerlessness. Many men and women who for
years felt quite content in their religious life are questioning
the meaning of their vocation. They wonder if they have
any real contribution to make and if the world really needs
them. They even wonder if they have not been misled by
dubious motives and false aspirations. Many ask themselves
if they ever made a truly free decision and if they were not
seduced by a type of pietism that now seems totally irrele-
vant.

In this context of self-doubt, many start experiencing a

deep sense of alienation and loneliness. Often they try to develop new life-styles within their own communities, but in doing so they discover how deep their real needs are and how hard it is to feel satisfied in their own houses. It is not surprising that deep sexual urges, which until then had remained beneath the threshold of consciousness, come to the center of awareness and often lead to a desire for a total break with the past and for a new way of life in which intimacy can be more directly experienced. Often those who are most sensitive to the fears and anger of our world and seek most intensely for solutions, also experience most deeply a need for affection and tenderness that their community cannot satisfy.

Thus we may wonder if many men and women in religious communities have not become so deeply affected by the fears and anger of our world that it has become practically impossible for them to be like children playing pipes and inviting others to dance (See Lk. 7:32). Their inner torments and restlessness have often reached such an intensity that their primary concern has become their own physical and emotional survival. This requires so much energy that a vital and convincing witness to God's loving and caring presence can hardly be expected of them.

All this suggests that a community in which no real intimacy can be experienced cannot be a creative witness for very long in our fearful and angry world. In this situation we need to take a very careful look at the importance of solitude in the life of a community. It might be that by de-emphasizing solitude in favor of the urgent needs of our world, we are endangering the very basis of our Christian witness. Hence I would like first of all to discuss solitude as the source of a lasting sense of intimacy.

Free from compulsions

Solitude is the place where we can reach the profound bond that is deeper than the emergency bonds of fear and anger. Although fear and anger can indeed drive us together, they cannot give rise to a common witness. In solitude we can come to the realization that we are not driven together but brought together. In solitude we come to know our fellow human beings not as partners who can satisfy our deepest needs, but as brothers and sisters with whom we are called to give visibility to God's all-embracing love. In solitude we discover that community is not a common ideology, but a response to a common call. In solitude we indeed realize that community is not made but given.

Solitude, then, is not private time in contrast to time together, nor a time to restore our tired minds. Solitude is very different from a time-out from community life. Solitude is the ground from which community grows. When we pray alone, study, read, write, or simply spend quiet time away from the places where we interact with each other directly, we enter into a deeper intimacy with each other. It is a fallacy to think that we grow closer to each other only when we talk, play, or work together. Much growth certainly occurs in such human interactions, but these interactions derive their fruit from solitude, because in solitude our intimacy with each other is deepened. In solitude we discover each other in a way that physical presence makes difficult if not impossible. There we recognize a bond with each other that does not depend on words, gestures, or actions, a bond much deeper than our own efforts can create.

If we base our life together on our physical proximity, on our ability to spend time together, speak with each other, eat together, and worship together, community life quickly starts fluctuating according to moods, personal attractiveness, and mutual compatibility, and thus will become very demanding and tiring. Solitude is essential for community life because there we begin to discover a unity that is prior to all unifying actions. In solitude we become aware that we were together before we came together and that community life is not a creation of our will but an obedient response to the reality of our being united. Whenever we enter into solitude, we witness to a love that transcends our interpersonal communications and proclaims that we love each other because we have been loved first (1 Jn. 4:19). Solitude keeps us in touch with the sustaining love from which community draws its strength. It sets us free from the compulsions of fear and anger and allows us to be in the midst of an anxious and violent world as a sign of hope and a source of courage. In short, solitude creates that free community that makes bystanders say, "See how they love each other."

A chaste love

This view of solitude as the fertile ground of community has very practical implications. It means that time for silence, individual study, personal prayer, and meditation must be seen to be as important to all the members of the community as acting together, working together, playing together, and worshiping together.

I am deeply convinced that gentleness, tenderness, peacefulness, and the inner freedom to move closer to one another, or to withdraw from one another, are nurtured in solitude. Without solitude we begin to cling to each other; we begin to worry about what we think and feel about each other; we quickly become suspicious of one another or irritated with each other; and we begin, often in unconscious ways, to scrutinize each other with a tiring hypersensitivity. Without solitude shallow conflicts easily grow deep and cause painful wounds. Then "talking things out" can become a burdensome obligation and daily life becomes so self-conscious that long-term living together is virtually impossible. Without solitude we will always suffer from a gnawing question about more or less: "Does he love me more than she does? Is our love today less than it was yesterday?"

These questions easily lead to divisions, tensions, apprehensions, and mutual irritability. Without solitude communities quickly become cliques.

With solitude, however, we learn to depend on God, by whom we are called together in love, in whom we can rest, and through whom we can enjoy and trust one another even when our ability to express ourselves to each other is limited. With solitude we are protected against the harmful effects of mutual suspicions, and our words and actions can become joyful expressions of an already existing trust rather than a subtle way of asking for proof of trustworthiness. With solitude we can experience each other as different manifestations of a love that transcends all of us.

> *This explains why solitude affects our sexual needs. Solitude prevents us from relating to our sexuality as a way to prove that we can love and thus liberates it from its compulsive quality. It allows us to experience our sexual feelings as a manifestation of God's unconditional love. In solitude a free response to our sexual identity becomes possible and sexual abstinence can indeed become a real option for men and women dedicated to the religious life.*

Solitude then becomes the place where chastity finds its roots. Chastity obviously means much more than sexual abstinence. It is the gentle guide to all forms of intimacy. Chastity leads to the intimate knowledge of God's effective love for us and sets us free to develop creative relationships in our world without being caught by its many "oughts" and "musts." Chastity makes intimacy possible by freeing it from its worldly compulsiveness.

Solitude, thus, is essential to community life because it liberates us from the power of fear and anger and offers a sense of intimacy that transcends the emergencies of our present-day world. It offers hope by making people say with a new amazement: "See how they love one another."

SOLITUDE AND MINISTRY

The individualization of ministries

Having seen how, in our emergency-oriented world, solitude can indeed deepen the communal witness of love, we now have to explore how solitude also strengthens the communal witness of service. One of the most obvious reponses to an emergency situation is that people give up their long-range goals and focus on the most pressing problems. When a city or town is being bombed, doctors stop their research on complex medical problems and give first aid to the wounded. When a sense of emergency begins to pervade a culture, short-term solutions, provisional care, and temporary aid easily obscure the need for carefully studied long-term projects.

I wonder if much of the ministry of religious communities has not been deeply affected by this sense of emergency. Forms of ministry to which many communities were committed for decades have suddenly lost their appeal to many of their members. Teaching ministries, hospital ministries, and many other traditional forms of ministry no longer seem to be responses to the urgent needs of the times, and many religious communities find themselves in the process of re-evaluation and reorientation. In the midst of this search for new relevance, it has become very hard for religious communities to present their ministry as a communal ministry.

The question, "What is the special vocation of your community?" is often difficult to answer. Mostly the response is, "Some of us work in hospitals, some teach, some work in a parish, a few of us have individual apostolates, and together we try to support each other in our different vocations." The great gain is obviously the wide variety of ministries that have become available: ministries to prisoners, to drug addicts, to shut-ins, to gay people; ministries in parishes, in factories, in mental institutions; also ministries that focus on music, art, or the media. The deinstitutionalization of religious life has opened up an enormous range of ministerial options that, not too long ago, were practically taboo for many men and women living in religious houses.

But there is also a loss involved, and that is the loss of the communal character of the Christian ministry. Often it seems that our ministries have become so individualized that it has become very hard to give a convincing visibility to our ministry as a common task. The emphasis on the particular talents of the individuals has made it very hard sometimes to speak about a ministry of the community. Often we can only speak about the ministries of its members.

I wonder if, by this individualization of our ministries, we have not lost the possibility of being a common witness. As religious communities, we not only have to serve individual people and their concrete needs, but we must also be a sign of courage and confidence to the larger society. Precisely in a culture so ripped apart by emergencies, it is not enough to minister to the many wounded individuals, but it is urgent also to offer hope to the many who are not directly touched by us, but who see our common ministry and say: "See how they serve their neighbor." The great power of a common vocation is that by its special visibility as a communal vocation it can touch, heal, and inspire many more than those who are directly affected by it.

> *Personally I have found enormous strength in the witness of the Taizé community although I have never been there. I have found great hope in the work of Jean Vanier although I have never met him. I have found much comfort in just knowing about the work and life of the Little Brothers and Little Sisters, the Missionaries of Charity, and the San Egidio Community. These communal ministries have prevented me from joining the many pessimistic voices.*

It is the communal ministry that is so crucial in our time, and needs to be of great concern to us.

A common vocation

What has all this to do with solitude? Solitude is the place where religious communities find their communal identity. It is the place where as members of a religious community we can listen to God's call and discern our common vocation. Why is this the case? Isn't solitude the place where we are with God and God alone, and where we can come to understand our own most individual call? Yes, but not in contrast to a common vocation. Because in solitude we can recognize how we can put our most personal talents in the service of a common task. It is very naïve to think that our individual giftedness can be directly translated into a call. To say, "I can write well, so God wants me to be a writer; I can teach well, so God wants me to be a teacher; I can play the piano well, so God wants me to be a pianist," makes us forget that our own self-understanding is not necessarily God's understanding of us. There was a time in which a one-sided view of humility led to the negation or denial of individual gifts. Hopefully, that time is gone. But to think that individual gifts are the manifestation of God's will reveals a one-sided view of vocation and obscures the fact that our talents can be as much the way to God as *in the way of* God.

In solitude we take some distance from the many opinions and ideas of our fellow human beings and become vulnerable to God. There we can listen carefully to him and distinguish between our desires and our task, between our urges and our vocation, between the cravings of our heart and the call of God. I have the sense that in communities where solitude is not an integral part of daily life we quickly start becoming deaf to God's demands and become mostly concerned with doing "my thing," without much thought about our communal task. Then communities become little more than mutual support groups in which the awareness of a common task has moved to the background of our consciousness.

Solitude is the place where our common vocation becomes visible. We should never forget that God calls us as a people, and that our individual religious vocations should always be seen as a part of the larger vocation of the community. We cannot use the community as a means to develop or give shape to our individual religious aspirations. As long as we see the community as a support system to help us realize our individual ideals, we are more children of our time than children of God. Our own individual vocation can only be seen as a particular manifestation of the vocation of the community to which we belong.

Solitude is precisely the ground where this common vocation becomes manifest. There we can empty ourselves of our needs for self-affirmation, self-realization, and self-fulfillment and begin to experience how God's call comes to us through the brothers and sisters with whom we live. The deep love of our community will then lead us constantly to consider how our ministry can be an expression of the ministry to which we are called together.

The obedient community

This view of solitude as the place where our common ministerial task can be discerned has some very concrete implications. It implies that obedience, as listening to God's call, is a central task of the community as a whole and cannot be reduced to the relationship of individual members to their superior. Obedience to the superior can only be experienced as real listening to God when it is experienced as an integral part of the listening of the whole community. This communal obedience is obviously not a simple act. Rather it is a way of life in which, as members of a community, we keep returning to solitude in order to become more sensitive to the ways in which God calls us here and now.

Thus, it is a sad development when retreats, days of recollection, or hours of meditation are simply left to the initiative of the individual. It is a sign of real maturity when the members of a community have a genuine desire to enter into solitude together and share regularly with each other the fruit of their prayers, meditations, and studies. Being alone with God for yourself is a very different experience from being alone with God as part of your life together. I am deeply convinced that great renewal will develop wherever communities enter regularly into solitude to discover together where God is calling them. No important decision, no important change in direction should ever be made without periods of long, silent listening in which all members are participating in some way.

I might also mention the importance of regular silence in community life. Silence as a simple rule can be very, very fruitless—but silence as the way in which we listen together to God's presence in our midst and open ourselves to his guidance is an indispensable element in a healthy community life. During the last years so much emphasis has been put on words in the form of conferences, study days, and sharing sessions that it seems important to deepen our realization that words can only bear fruit when they are born in silence. Especially in periods of crises, conflicts, and strong emotional tensions, silence can not only offer healing but also show new ways for our life together.

Solitude then is the place of communal obedience. Especially in a time of emergency, in which the ability to meet constant change is a necessary quality of the contemporary community, a deep commitment to solitude is crucial. You can practically judge the health of a religious community by its commitment to solitude. Ministry in a world of ongoing change needs to be deeply rooted in a quiet, silent encounter with our faithful God. This allows the community to move quickly and efficiently when the day or the hour asks for it, without having the sense of interruption or disruption. This also makes it possible for a diversity of concrete tasks to be experienced and seen as different manifestations of a common ministry. In solitude their unity can be discerned and continually strengthened and nurtured.

When we as communities are indeed deeply in touch with God, who calls us to a task in this world, then it will be possible to live in an emergency-oriented world and respond creatively to the concrete events of the day without being seduced into panic reactions or erratic movements. Then we can prevent the emergencies from throwing us back on ourselves in self-protective or self-serving actions, and then we can perform a ministry of hope that makes people say with amazement: "See how they serve their neighbor."

SOLITUDE AND PRAYER

Religious secularism

Just as solitude affects our mutual love and our common ministry, so too has solitude a deep influence on our relationship with God. The witness of Christian community not only makes people say: "See how they love one another" and "See how they serve their neighbor," but also "See how they pray to their Lord."

It is very simplistic to say that emergencies make people pay more attention to God and reawaken religious feelings. We might in fact wonder if the opposite is not more often the case. Fear and anger do not lead to God. The great pressures of our time have created much bitterness, resentment, and hatred. Many people have turned away from God and prayer since they no longer see how they can pray to a God who allows so much cruelty, so much agony, so much pain.

Religious communities have certainly not remained immune to this. In fact, I have a strong feeling that as religious people, we have come to relate to God in a very ambivalent way.

Our relationship to God has come very close to a love-hate relationship. We may often ask ourselves, "Can God really be trusted, does he really love us, does he really care?" Although we seldom will question this with words, our behavior often betrays us. We say to friends, "I will pray for you," but we seldom consider that a serious commitment. We listen to lectures affirming the importance of prayer, but we really think that our people need actions and not prayer and that praying is good when you really have nothing else to do. I wonder if under the surface of our religiosity we do not have great doubts about God's effectiveness in our world, about his interest in us—yes, even about his presence among us. I wonder if many of us are not plagued by deep, hostile feelings toward God and the idea of God without having any way to express them. I even wonder if there are many religious people for whom God is their only concern.

When we speak of our age as a secular age, we must first of all be willing to become aware of how deeply this secularism has entered into our own hearts and how doubt, hesitation, suspicion, anger, and even hatred corrode our relationship with God.

In many, if not most, religious communities prayer has lost its central place, not only because of changing conditions in our milieu, but also because God himself has become a very dubious partner, someone with whom you have to stay friends to avoid problems, but whose presence you hardly enjoy. Although for most religious people these feelings and experiences keep lingering on the threshold of their consciousness, a few reach the point in which they experience themselves as cowards who lack the courage to let God go and live their own lives. This feeling of cowardice reveals a sense of being caught by God in a net of fear and dependency and often leads to self-destructive anger.

In many of our religious communities God has become little more than the silver frame for our own pictures. Beautiful liturgies, insightful conferences, and occasional retreats are considered very inspiring in our lives together, but somewhere—often deep down—we know that without them things would hardly be different. It is, therefore, not surprising that many people have left religious life rather easily, often with the sensation that emotional, as well as physical, chains have been taken away from them and that they can now do better what they did well before.

This is not meant as an indictment. On the contrary. The religious secularism that I have described has entered so deeply into our way of being in the world that it cannot be subject to simple accusations. But it can be made subject to reflection, because it not only shows how closely we, as religious people, have become part of our emergency-oriented world, but it also explains why it has become difficult for our contemporary religious communities to be unambiguous witnesses to the living God.

The great encounter

It is in the context of this religious secularism that solitude receives its deepest meaning, because solitude is the place where God reveals himself as God-with-us, as the God

who is our creator, redeemer, and sanctifier, as the God who
is the source, the center and the purpose of our existence, as
the God who wants to give himself to us with an unconditional, unlimited, and unrestrained love, and as the
God who wants to be loved by us with all our heart, all
our soul, and all our mind. Solitude indeed is the place of
the great encounter, from which all other encounters derive
their meaning. In solitude, we meet God. In solitude, we
leave behind our many activities, concerns, plans and projects, opinions and convictions, and enter into the presence
of our loving God, naked, vulnerable, open, and receptive.
And there we see that he alone is God, that he alone is
love, that he alone is care, that he alone is forgiveness. In
solitude we indeed can call God our Father, the loving
Father of all people.

I am not saying this to suggest that there is an easy solution to our ambivalent relationship with God. Solitude is not
a solution. It is a direction. The direction is pointed to by
the prophet Elijah, who did not find Yahweh in the mighty
wind, the earthquake, the fire, but in the still small voice;
this direction, too, is indicated by Jesus, who chose solitude
as the place to be with his Father. Every time we enter into
solitude we withdraw from our windy, earthquaking, fiery
lives and open ourselves to the great encounter. The first
thing we often discover in solitude is our own restlessness,
our drivenness and compulsiveness, our urge to act quickly,
to make an impact, and to have influence; and often we find

it very hard to withstand the temptation to return as quickly as possible to the world of "relevance." But when we persevere with the help of a gentle discipline, we slowly come to hear the still, small voice and to feel the gentle breeze, and so come to know the Lord of our heart, soul, and mind, the Lord who makes us see who we really are.

Here we touch the greatest gift of solitude. It is the gift of a new self, a new identity. Solitude leads us to a new intimacy with each other and makes us see our common task precisely because in solitude we discover our true nature, our true self, our true identity. That knowledge of who we really are allows us to live and work in community. As long as our life and work together are based on a false or distorted self-understanding, we are bound to become entangled in interpersonal conflict and to lose perspective on our common task.

This leads us to take another look at our fear and anger. While fear and anger are the most "natural" and most "obvious" reactions to a state of emergency, they have to be unmasked as expressions of our false selves. When we are trembling with fear or seething with anger, we have sold our soul to the world or to a false God. Fear and anger take our freedom away and make us victims of the powers that surround us. Fear, as well as anger, reveal how deeply our sense of worth has become dependent on our success in the world and on the opinions of others, and how we have become what we do or what others think of us.

In solitude, however, fear and anger can slowly be unmasked as manifestations of a false self, and in solitude they can lose their power in the embrace of God's love. That is what St. John means when he says: "In love there can be no fear, but fear is driven out by perfect love" (1 Jn. 4:18). In solitude we can gradually be led to the truth that we are who God made us to be. Therefore, solitude is a place of conversion. There we are converted from people who want to show each other what we have and what we can do into people who raise our open and empty hands to God in the recognition that all we are is a free gift from God. Thus, in solitude, we not only encounter God but also our true self. In fact, it is precisely in the light of God's presence that we can see who we really are. To the degree that we know God and know ourselves through him, we come together not as a group of individuals huddling together out of fear or driven together by a common anger, but as a community of people who can freely witness to the presence of God in the midst of this world.

Empty before God

When we see solitude as the place of the great encounter, the place where we know God as the loving Father and ourselves as the people able to respond fully to his love without fear and anger, then we know that solitude is indeed the place of prayer. Prayer is the breath of the Christian community. With a false view of God and a mistaken self-identity, prayer is not possible and community life slowly suffocates.

In this final section, I would like to emphasize the importance of intercessory prayer. If it is true that solitude diverts us from our fears and anger and makes us empty for God, then it is also true that precisely in solitude an enormous space opens up into which we can welcome all the people of the world. There is a powerful connection between poverty and intercessory prayer. When we give up what sets us apart from others—not just property but also opinions, prejudices, judgments, and mental preoccupations—then we can allow friends as well as enemies to enter with us into our solitude and lift them up to God in the midst of the great encounter. In real solitude there is an unlimited space for others, because there we are empty and there we can see that, in fact, nobody stands over and against us. An enemy is only our enemy as long as we have something to defend. But when we have nothing to hold onto, nothing to protect, nothing to consider as exclusively ours, then nobody can be an enemy and then we can, in fact, recognize in the center of our solitude that all men and women are brothers and sisters. In solitude, we stand so naked and so vulnerable before God, and become so deeply aware of our total dependency on his love, that not only our friends but also those who kill, lie, torture, rape, and wage wars can become part of our flesh and blood. In solitude we are so totally poor that we can enter into solidarity with all human beings and allow our hearts to become the place of encounter not only with God, but, through God, with all human beings as well. And thus intercessory prayer is the prayer of self-emptying because it asks of us to give up all that divides us from others so that we can *become* those we pray for and let God touch them in us.

Thus we see how, through prayer and especially through intercessory prayer, the religious community stands open to the whole world. By their prayers, the members of a religious community form a circle as open as St. Peter's square where there is space for anyone and everyone. Often we are painfully aware of how little we can do to help the people of this world in their immense needs. But maybe we would be less pessimistic if we could live our limited actions as expressions of unlimited prayer. We may lose courage and confidence if we measure our value by counting those who are deeply affected by our actions, but when we remain aware of the countless people who can be embraced by our prayers, we can live joyfully and gratefully.

The prayer of the religious community belongs to the core of its witness and it is, therefore, a sign of hope when people say not only, "See how they love one another" and "See how they serve their neighbor," but also "See how they pray to their Lord."

CONCLUSION

This brings me to the conclusion of this reflection on the relationship between solitude and community life. Let me now summarize.

First of all, I have tried to demonstrate how deeply the state of emergency in which our world finds itself has affected the life of our religious communities. Our interpersonal relationships have been tainted by fear and anger; our common tasks have been threatened by fragmentation and individualization; and our prayer has often lost its central place in our daily life together. Second, I have pointed to solitude, not as the simple solution to these problems, but as a place from where a response to the emergencies of our time can be made. I have described solitude as the place where mature intimacy can develop between people, as the place where we can discover or rediscover our common vocation, and as the place where our great encounter with God can take place. Thus I have tried to show that solitude is the foundation of our life in community. Finally, I wanted to help you see that the exploration of the role of solitude in our lives together offers a context for a new perspective on the contemporary meaning of chastity, obedience, and poverty. Solitude makes us experience God's love as the source of all human love and thus makes us see that chastity is the guide for our intimate relationships with each other. Solitude makes us obedient to the call of God to a communal life, and solitude asks us to become poor and so to create a free space where all the suffering people in the world can be received and lifted up in unceasing prayer. Thus solitude is the ground on which chastity, obedience, and poverty can blossom and become rich gifts to the religious community.

I hope that I have been able to convince you of the indispensability of solitude in the life of the religious community. As we approach the end of our millennium, let us deepen our commitment to solitude so that, surrounded by many apocalyptic events, we can give visibility to God's faithfulness and lead many people to the hopeful observations: "See how they love one another; see how they serve their neighbor; see how they pray to their Lord."

CHAPTER II

Celibacy and the Holy

INTRODUCTION

When you look out over the city of Rome, walk in its
streets, or ride in its buses, you quickly realize that it is a
crowded city full of houses, full of people, full of cars, yes—
even full of cats. You see men and women moving quickly in
all directions, you hear joyful and angry voices mixed with a
great variety of street sounds, you smell many odors—
especially cappuccino—and you feel the Italian embrace by
which you gain a friend or lose your money. It is a busy,
congested city, in which life manifests itself in all its boister-
ous intensity.

But in the midst of this lively and colorful conglomeration
of houses, people, and cars, there are the domes of Rome
pointing to the places set apart for the Holy One. The
churches of Rome are like beautiful frames around empty
spaces witnessing to him who is the quiet, still center of all
human life. The churches are not useful, not practical, not
requiring immediate action or quick response. They are
spaces without loud noises, hungry movements, or impa-
tient gestures. They are tranquil spaces, strangely empty
most of the time. They speak a language different from the
world around them. They do not want to be museums. They
want to invite us to be silent, to sit or kneel, to listen attentively, and to rest with our whole being.

A city without carefully protected empty spaces where

one can sense the silence from which all words grow, and rest in the stillness from which all actions flow, such a city is in danger of losing its real center.

I wonder if the busy city with its many quiet places cannot offer us an image of what celibacy might mean in our contemporary society. After all, isn't the active street life that part of us that wants to be with others, to move and to produce, and isn't the dome carefully protecting some empty space that other part of us that needs to be protected and even defended to prevent our lives from losing their center? Our inner sanctum, that inner, holy place, that sacred center in our lives where only God may enter, that is as important for our lives as the domes are for the city of Rome. Much can be said about celibacy. But I want to reflect on it from just one perspective. I want to look at celibacy as a witness to the inner sanctum in our own lives and in the lives of others. By giving a special visibility to this inner sanctum, this holy, empty space in human life, the celibate man or woman wants to affirm and proclaim that all human intimacy finds its deepest meaning and fulfillment when it is experienced and lived as a participation in the intimacy of God himself.

In order to explore the meaning of the witness of the celibate life, I would like to focus on three areas: first on the world in which celibacy is lived; then on the nature of the witness that the celibate offers to this world; and finally on the life-style by which this witness is enhanced and strengthened.

THE WORLD

The limits of the interpersonal

The world in which celibacy wants to be a witness for a holy, empty space is a world that puts great emphasis on interpersonal relationships. We can safely say that in the Western culture of the last few decades the value of coming together, being together, living together, and loving together has received more attention than ever before. The healing power of eye contact, of attentive listening, and of the careful touch has been explored by many psychologists, sensitivity trainers, and communication experts. Practically every year you can hear about a new type of therapy, a new form of consciousness enlarging, or a new method of communication. Many, many people suffering from feelings of isolation, alienation, or loneliness have found new hope and strength in these experiments in togetherness. Just seeing the great popularity and the growing influence of re-evaluation therapy is enough to convince a sympathetic observer that a deep need is being responded to.

We indeed need each other and are able to give each other much more than we often realize. Too long have we been burdened by fear and guilt, and too long have we denied each other the affection and closeness we rightly desire. We, therefore, have much to learn from those who are trying to open up new and more creative interpersonal relations.

But critical questions still need to be raised. Can real intimacy be reached without a deep respect for that holy place within and between us, that space that should remain untouched by human hands? Can human intimacy really be fulfilling when every space within and between us is being filled up? Is the emphasis on the healing possibilities of human togetherness not often the result of a one-sided perception of our human predicament? These questions have a new urgency in the time of the human-potential movements. I often wonder if we do not think or feel that our painful experiences of loneliness are primarily results of a lack of interpersonal closeness. We seem to think: "If I could just break through my fear to express my real feelings of love and hostility, if I could just feel free to hold a friend, if I could just talk honestly and openly with my own people. If I could just live with someone who really cares . . . then I would have again some inner peace and experience again some inner wholeness." When any of these experiences have become reality to us we feel, in fact, a certain relief, but the question remains if it is there that the real source of our healing and wholeness can be found. In a world in which traditional patterns of human communications have broken down and in which family, profession, or village no longer offer the intimate bonds they did in the past, the basic human condition of aloneness has entered so deeply into our emotional awareness that we are constantly tempted to want more from our fellow human beings than they can give. If we relate to our neighbors with the supposition that they are able to fulfill our deepest needs, we will find ourselves increasingly frustrated, because, when we expect a friend or lover to be able to take away our deepest pain, we expect from him or her something that cannot be given by human beings. No human being can understand us fully, no human being can give us unconditional love, no human being can offer constant affection, no human being can enter into the core of our being and heal our deepest brokenness. When we forget that and expect from others more than they can give, we will be quickly disillusioned; for when we do not receive what we expect, we easily become resentful, bitter, revengeful, and even violent.

Lately we have become very much aware of the fragile border between intimacy and violence. We see or hear about cruelty between husband and wife, parents and children, brothers and sisters, and start realizing that those who desire so desperately to be loved, find themselves often entangled in violent relationships. The stories in the daily paper about sexual aggression, mutilation, and murder evoke the vision of people desperately grasping each other and clinging to each other, crying out and shouting for love, but not receiving anything but more violence.

Spinoza's words, "Nature abhors a vacuum," seem quite applicable to us, and the temptation is indeed very great to take flight into an intimacy and closeness that does not leave any open space. Much suffering results from this suffocating closeness.

With praying hands

I found a good image to describe our predicament in the book *Existential Metapsychiatry* by New York psychiatrist Thomas Hora (New York: Seabury Press, 1977, p. 32). Thomas Hora calls the great emphasis on interpersonal relationships as the way to healing *personalism,* and he compares this personalism with the interlocking fingers of two hands. The fingers of the two hands can intertwine only to the point that a stalemate is reached. After that the only possible movement is backward, causing friction and eventually pain. And too much friction leads to separation. When we relate to each other as the interlocking fingers of two hands we enter into a suffocating closeness that does not leave any free space. When lonely people with a strong desire for intimacy move closer and closer to each other in the hope of coming to an experience of belonging and wholeness, all too frequently they find themselves locked in a situation in which closeness leads to friction, friction to pain, and pain to separation.

Many marriages are so short-lived precisely because there

is an intense desire for closeness and a minimal amount of space that allows for free movement. Because of the high emotional expectation with which they enter into a relationship, married couples often panic when they do not experience the inner contentment for which they had hoped. Often they try very hard to alleviate their tensions by exploring in much detail their life together, only to end up in a stalemate, tired, exhausted, and finally forced to separate in order to avoid mutual harm.

Thomas Hora suggests as the image for a true human relationship two hands coming together parallel in a prayerful gesture, pointing beyond themselves and moving freely in relation to one another. I find this a helpful image exactly because it makes it clear that a mature human intimacy requires a deep and profound respect for the free and empty space that needs to exist within and between partners and that asks for a continuous mutual protection and nurture. Only in this way can a relationship be lasting, precisely because mutual love is experienced as a participation in a greater and earlier love to which it points. In this way intimacy can be rich and fruitful, since it has been given carefully protected space in which to grow. This relationship no longer is a fearful clinging to each other but a free dance, allowing space in which we can move forward and backward, form constantly new patterns, and see each other as always new.

The world in which we live is a world with many fearful,

lonely, and anxious people clinging to each other to find some relief, some satisfaction, and some joy. The tragedy of our world is that much of the intense desire for love, acceptance, and belonging is cruelly turned into jealousy, resentment, and violence, often to the bitter surprise of those who had no other desire than to live in peace and love.

In this world with many people anxiously clinging to each other, a sign of hope needs to be given. In this world celibacy, as a visible manifestation of the holy space in an overcrowded world, can be a powerful witness in service of mature human relationships.

THE WITNESS

Vacancy for God

The best definition of celibacy, I think, is the definition of Thomas Aquinas. Thomas calls celibacy a vacancy for God. To be a celibate means to be empty for God, to be free and open for his presence, to be available for his service. This view on celibacy, however, has often led to the false idea that being empty for God is a special privilege of celibates, while other people involved in all sorts of interpersonal relationships are not empty but full, occupied as well as pre-occupied. If we look at celibacy as a state of life that upholds the importance of God's presence in our lives in contrast with other states of life that lead to entanglement in worldly affairs, we quickly slip into a dangerous elitism considering celibates as domes rising up amid the many low houses of the city.

I think that celibacy can never be considered as a special prerogative of a few members of the people of God. Celibacy, in its deepest sense of creating and protecting emptiness for God, is an essential part of all forms of Christian life: marriage, friendship, single life, and community life. We will never fully understand what it means to be celibate unless we recognize that celibacy is, first of all, an element, and even an essential element in the life of all Christians. Let me illustrate how this is true in marriage and friendship.

Marriage is not a lifelong attraction of two individuals to each other, but a call for two people to witness together to God's love. The basis of marriage is not mutual affection, or feelings, or emotions and passions that we associate with love, but a vocation, a being elected to build together a house for God in this world, to be like the two cherubs whose outstretched wings sheltered the Ark of the Covenant and created a space where Yahweh could be present (Ex. 25:10–12, 1 Ki. 8:6–7). Marriage is a relationship in which a man and a woman protect and nurture the inner sanctum within and between them and witness to that by the way in which they love each other. Marriage, too, is therefore a *vacare Deo*. Celibacy is part of marriage not simply because married couples may have to be able to live separated from each other for long periods of time, because they may need to abstain from sexual relations for physical, mental, or spiritual reasons, but also because the intimacy of marriage itself is an intimacy that is based on the common participation in a love greater than the love two people can offer each other. The real mystery of marriage is not that husband and wife love each other so much that they can find God in each other's lives, but that God loves them so much that they can discover each other more and more as living reminders of his divine presence. They are brought together, indeed, as two prayerful hands extended toward God and forming in this way a home for him in this world.

The same thing is true for friendship. Deep and mature

friendship does not mean that we keep looking each other in the eyes and are constantly impressed or enraptured by each other's beauty, talents, and gifts, but it means that together we look at him who calls us to his service.

I was deeply impressed by the way the members of the San Egidio community in Trastevere described their relationship with each other. They made it very clear to me that friendship is very important to them, but that they have to learn in their apostolate to keep seeing their relationships with each other in the context of their common call. As soon as the relationship itself becomes central they are moving away from their vocation. They have to be willing to let new developments in their apostolate separate them from each other for certain periods of time, and they also have to be willing to see and experience their separations as an invitation to deepen their relationship with their Lord and through him with each other. That is why they feel so strongly that their weekly Eucharist and their daily vespers form the source of their love for each other. There they find each other as friends, there they strengthen their commitment to each other, and there they find the courage to follow their Lord even when he asks them to go in different directions. Thus their relationship is really a standing together around the altar or around the holy empty space indicated by the icon. Together they want to protect the empty space in and between each other.

Thus marriage and friendship carry within their center a holy vacancy, a space that is for God and God alone. Without that holy center, marriage as well as friendship become like a city without domes, a city forgetting the meaning and direction of its own activities.

Living reminders

We can now see that celibacy has a very important place in our world. The celibate makes his life into a visible witness for the priority of God in our lives, a sign to remind all people that without the inner sanctum our lives lose contact with their source and goal. We belong to God. All people do. Celibates are people who, by not attaching themselves to any one particular person, remind us that the relationship with God is the beginning, the source, and the goal of all human relationships.

By his or her life of nonattachment, the celibate lifts up an aspect of the Christian life of which we all need to be reminded. The celibate is like the clown in the circus who, between the scary acts of the trapeze artists and lion tamers, fumbles and falls, reminding us that all human activities are ultimately not so important as the virtuosi make us believe. Celibates live out the holy emptiness in their lives by not marrying, by not trying to build for themselves a house or a fortune, by not trying to wield as much influence as possible, and by not filling their lives with events, people, or creations for which they will be remembered. They hope that by their empty lives God will be recognized as the source of all human thoughts and actions. Especially by not marrying and by abstaining from the most intimate expression of human love, the celibate becomes a living sign of the limits of interpersonal relationships and of the centrality of the inner sanctum that no human being may violate.

To whom, then, is this witness directed? I dare to say that celibacy is, first of all, a witness to all those who are married. I wonder if we have explored enough the very important relationship between marriage and celibacy. Lately we have become aware of this interrelatedness in a very painful way. The crisis of celibacy and the crisis of married life appeared together. At the same time that many priests and religious persons move away from the celibate life, we see many couples questioning the value of their commitment to each other. These two phenomena, although they are not connected with each other as cause and effect, are closely related because marriage and celibacy are two ways of living within the Christian community that support each other. Celibacy is a support to married people in their commitment to each other. The celibate reminds those who live together in marriage of their own celibate center, which they need to protect and nurture in order to live a life that does not depend simply upon the stability of emotions and affections, but also on their common love for God, who called them together. On the other hand, married people also witness to those who have chosen the celibate life, reminding them that it is the love of God that indeed makes rich and creative human relationships possible and that the value of the celibate life becomes manifest in a generous, affectionate, and faithful care for those in need. Married people remind celibates that celibates also live in covenant and are brides and grooms. Thus celibacy and marriage need each other.

Celibates can indeed have a very good understanding of married life and married people of celibate life. Remarks such as: "You don't know what you are talking about because you are not married (or celibate)" can be very misleading. Precisely because marriage and celibacy are in each other's service and bound together by their common witness to God's love as the love from which all human relationships originate, celibate and married people can be of invaluable help to each other by supporting their different life-styles.

Celibacy not only witnesses to the inner sanctum to married people, but also, together with marriage, celibacy speaks of the presence of God in the world to anyone who is there to listen. In a world so congested and so entangled in conflict and pain, celibates by their dedication to God in a single life-style, and married people by their dedication to God in a life together, are signs of God's presence in this world. They both ask us in different ways to turn to God as the source of all human relationships. They both say in different ways that without giving God his rightful place in the midst of the city, we all die in the hopeless attempt to fabricate peace and love by ourselves. The celibate speaks of the need to respect the inner sanctum at all cost; the married Christian speaks of the need to base human relationships on the intimacy with God himself. But both speak for God and his Lordship in the world, and together they give form to the Christian community and stand out as signs of hope.

Thus, in a world torn by loneliness and conflict and trying so hard to create better human relationships, celibacy is a very important witness. It encourages us to create space for him who sent his son, thus revealing to us that we can only love each other because he has loved us first.

THE LIFE-STYLE

Useless . . .

When we look at celibacy as a *vacare Deo,* a being empty for God as a visible witness for the inner sanctum in all people's lives, then it becomes clear that sexual abstinence can never be the most important aspect of celibacy. Not being married or not being involved in a sexual relationship does not constitute the celibate life. Celibacy is an openness to God of which sexual abstinence is only one of its manifestations. Celibacy is a life-style in which we try to witness to the priority of God in all relationships. This involves every part of our life, the way we eat and drink, work and play, sleep and rest, speak and be silent. It is an openness to God acted out in such a way that it must raise questions in those we encounter. It is a sort of lifelong street theater constantly trying to raise questions in people's minds about the deeper meaning of their own existence.

Therefore we need to see celibacy as a life-style in which we witness to God's place in this world in many ways other than sexual abstinence. I would like to discuss two aspects of celibacy that today are of special importance for a life-style that emphasizes life as a vacancy for God. They are contemplative prayer and voluntary poverty.

Contemplative prayer is an essential element of the celibate life, because it is first of all an attitude of being empty for God. Contemplative prayer is not a way of being busy with God instead of with people, but it is an attitude in which we recognize God's ultimate priority by being useless in his presence, by standing in front of him without anything to show, to prove, or to argue, and by allowing him to enter into our emptiness. Thus, an intimate connection exists between celibacy and contemplative prayer. Both are expressions of being vacant for God. In our utilitarian culture, in which we suffer from a collective compulsion to do something practical, helpful, or useful, and to make a contribution that can give us a sense of worth, contemplative prayer is a form of radical criticism. It is not useful or practical but a way of wasting time for God. It cuts a hole in our busyness and reminds us and others that it is God and not we who creates and sustains the world. Contemplative prayer as standing naked, powerless, and vulnerable before God, therefore, is one of the most important expressions of the celibate life-style.

In this useless prayer, God can show us his love. When we are empty, free, and open, we can be with him, look at him, listen to him, and slowly begin to realize that he is our loving Father who loves us with a deep, intimate affection. It is very important for a celibate to develop a very warm, affective, and intimate prayer life in which the gentle, caring love of God can be experienced and enjoyed. In this contemplative prayer we become really free, we sense that we are accepted, that we belong, that we are not totally alone but that we live in the embrace of him whose fatherhood includes motherly, brotherly, and sisterly love. Once we really know him in prayer then we can live in this world without a need to cling to anyone for self-affirmation, and then we can let the abundance of God's love be the source of all our ministry.

And poor . . .

Besides contemplative prayer, the celibate life-style also asks for voluntary poverty. A wealthy celibate is like a fat sprinter. Anyone who is serious about his celibacy has to ask himself, "Am I poor?" If the answer is, "No, I am much better off than most people, I can buy more than my parishioners, eat and drink better than those to whom I minister," then we have not yet taken our celibacy seriously. Voluntary poverty is probably one of the most important signs of a celibate life-style. In fact, many married people do not take celibacy seriously because they contrast their daily struggle to pay the bills for food, house, and education with the care-free life of celibates and wonder who is really living out the witness to the Gospel. If there is one aspect of contemporary ministry that needs emphasis today it is voluntary poverty. In a time in which we have become so aware of the sins of capitalism and hear daily about the millions who suffer from lack of food, shelter, and the most basic care, you cannot consider yourself a witness for God's presence when your own life is cluttered with material possessions, your belly overfull, and your mind crowded with worries about what to do with what you have. In our days voluntary poverty is probably the most necessary form of our vacancy for God. It is the most convincing sign of our solidarity with the world as we know it today, and the most powerful support for a life of sexual abstinence. Wherever the Church is vital, it is poor. It is true in Rome: Look at the work of the Missionaries of Charity, and at the Little Sisters and Brothers. It is true in Latin America: Look at the new forms of ministry in Mexico, Paraguay, and Brazil. It is true, too, in the United States: Look at the *Catholic Worker* and the Sojourners Community.

Wherever the Church renews itself it embraces voluntary poverty as a spontaneous response to the situation in this world, a response that expresses criticism of the growing wealth of the few and solidarity with the growing misery of the many.

What this poverty means concretely in the life of each of us is hard to say because this needs to be discerned in everyone's individual life. But I dare say that anyone who practices contemplative prayer in a disciplined way will be confronted sooner or later with Christ's words to the rich young man. Because if one thing is sure it is that we are all rich young men asking, "Teacher, what must I do to possess everlasting life?" It is not so clear yet that we are ready to hear the answer.

Thus we can say that contemplative prayer and voluntary poverty are the two main pillars that support a celibate life.

CONCLUSION

Trying to summarize and conclude these thoughts on celibacy, I am painfully aware that many questions you probably have about celibacy have hardly been touched. I have not discussed how our sexual drives, desires, and needs can be creatively integrated into a celibate life-style. I have not talked about the important relationship between celibacy and community life, and I have not spoken about the value of celibacy for a concrete day-to-day ministry. I wanted very consciously to avoid emphasizing the usefulness of celibacy. By speaking about celibacy as a way of life that makes us more available to our fellow human beings, that encourages us to share our gifts with many people, and that makes us more able to move freely to different places where the human needs ask most urgently for pastoral response . . . by speaking of celibacy in such a way I might make it too useful and take away too quickly the foolishness of making oneself a eunuch for the Kingdom of Heaven (see Mt. 19:12). Jesus did not present celibacy as a very practical, useful, and effective life-style. By saying about celibacy, "Let anyone accept this who can," he makes it clear that celibacy is not the most acceptable, understandable, or obvious choice in one's life. Making celibacy useful, therefore, would be more a tribute to the spirit of American pragmatism than to the spirit of the Gospel. To protect and nurture vacancy for God in the midst of a world that wants to offer self-fulfillment can hardly be useful or practical. Standing empty-handed in the presence of God is not useful, divesting oneself of possessions is not practical, and living a life without an intimate companion and without children is certainly not very smart.

But still, contemplative prayer, voluntary poverty, and sexual abstinence are three elements of a celibate life-style that together witness to the necessity of creating a vacancy where we can listen to God's voice and celebrate his presence in our midst. Only when we are willing to accept the uselessness, impracticality, and foolishness of this life-style may celibacy prove to be effective after all. But this type of effectiveness does not belong to the world. It belongs to the Kingdom of God. And this type of effectiveness can only be known when we have fully experienced the pain of our emptiness.

In the circus of life we indeed are the clowns. Let us train ourselves well so that those who watch us will smile and recognize that in the midst of our crowded city, we have to keep a place for him who loves his stubborn and hard-headed children with an infinite tenderness and care.

CHAPTER III

Prayer and Thought

INTRODUCTION

When we think about prayer, we usually regard it as one of the many things we do to live a full and mature Christian life. We say to ourselves or to each other, "We should not forget to pray because prayer is important; without it our life becomes shallow. We need to give our time not only to people, but to God as well." If we are fervent in our conviction that prayer is important, we might even be willing to give a whole hour to prayer every day, or a whole day every month, or a whole week every year. Thus prayer becomes a part, a very important part, of our life.

But when the apostle Paul speaks about prayer, he uses a very different language. He does not speak about prayer as a part of life, but as all of life. He does not mention prayer as something we should not forget, but claims it is our ongoing concern. He does not exhort his readers to pray once in a while, regularly, or often, but without hesitation admonishes them to pray constantly, unceasingly, without interruption. Paul does not ask us to spend some of every day in prayer. No, Paul is much more radical. He asks us to pray day and night, in joy and in sorrow, at work and at play, without intermissions or breaks. For Paul, praying is like breathing. It cannot be interrupted without mortal danger.

To the Christians in Thessalonica Paul writes: "Pray constantly, and for all things give thanks to God, because this is what God expects you to do in Christ Jesus" (1 Th. 5:17–18). Paul not only demands unceasing prayer but also practices it. "We constantly thank God for you" (1 Th. 2:13), he says to his community in Greece. "We feel we must be continually thanking God for you" (2 Th. 1:3). "We pray continually that our God will make you worthy of his call" (2 Th. 1:11). To the Romans he writes: "I never fail to mention you in my prayers" (Rm. 1:9), and he comforts his friend Timothy with the words: "Always I remember you in my prayers" (2 Tm. 1:3).

The two Greek terms that appear repeatedly in Paul's letters are *pantote* (always) and *adialeiptos* (without interruption). These words make it clear that for Paul, prayer is not a part of living, but all of living; not a part of his thought, but all of his thought; not a part of his emotions and feelings, but all of them. Paul's fervor allows no place for partial commitments, piecemeal giving, or hesitant generosity. He gives all and asks all.

This radicalism obviously raises some difficult questions. What does it mean to pray without ceasing? How can we live our lives with its many demands and obligations as an uninterrupted prayer? What about the endless row of distractions that intrude on us day after day? Moreover, how can our sleep, our needed moments of diversion, and the few hours in which we try to escape from the tensions and conflicts of life be lifted up into an unceasing prayer? These questions are real, and have puzzled many Christians who wanted to take seriously Paul's exhortation to pray without ceasing.

One of the best known examples of the desire for unceasing prayer is the nineteenth-century Russian peasant who wanted so much to be obedient to Paul's call for uninterrupted prayer that he went from staretz to staretz looking for an answer until he finally found a holy man who taught him the Jesus Prayer. He told the peasant to say thousands of times each day, "Lord Jesus Christ, have mercy on me." In this way, the Jesus Prayer slowly became united with his breathing and heartbeat so that he could travel through Russia carrying his knapsack with the Bible, the *Philokalia,* and some bread and salt, living a life of unceasing prayer (see *The Way of the Pilgrim,* translated from the Russian by R. M. French [New York: Seabury Press, 1965]). Although we are not nineteenth-century Russian peasants with a similar "wanderlust," we still share the question of this simple peasant: "How do we pray without ceasing?"

I would like to respond to this question not in the context of the wide, silent Russian steppes of the nineteenth century, but in the context of the restlessness of our contemporary Western society. I propose to look at unceasing prayer as the conversion of our unceasing thought processes. My central question, therefore, is, "How can we turn our perpetual mental activities into perpetual prayer?" or, to express it more simply, "How can thinking become praying?"

First I want to discuss how our unceasing thinking is the source of our joy as well as of our pain. Then I want to show how this unceasing thinking can be turned into an uninterrupted conversation with God. Finally I would like to explore how we can develop a discipline that will promote this ongoing conversion from thought to prayer. In this way, I hope that unceasing prayer can be removed from the sphere of romantic sentimentalism and become a realistic possibility for our demanding lives in the twentieth century.

UNCEASING THOUGHTS

Thinking reeds

Lately I have been wondering if we ever do *not* think. It seems to me that we are always involved in some kind of thought process and that being without thoughts is not a real human option. When Blaise Pascal calls a human being a *roseau pensant* (thinking reed), he indicates that our ability to think constitutes our humanity and that it is our thinking that sets us apart from all other created beings. All our emotions, passions, and feelings are intimately connected with our thoughts. We can even say that our thoughts form the cradle in which our joys as well as our sorrows are born. The words "thoughts" and "thinking" are used here in a very broad sense and include different mental processes. When we look at these different mental processes it appears that whether we like it or not, we are involved in, or subjected to, unceasing thoughts.

One of the forms of thinking with which we are most familiar, but which represents only a small part of our mental processes, is reflective thinking. Reflection is a conscious bending back over events or the ideas, images, and emotions connected with these events. It requires the application of our will power in a concentrated effort; it calls for discipline, endurance, patience, and much mental energy. Those who study a great deal know how hard systematic reflection is and how it can tire us and even exhaust us. Reflection is real work and does not come easily.

But not reflecting does not mean not thinking. In fact, we quite often find ourselves thinking without even realizing it.

> *You might be walking through the streets of Rome and find yourself thinking about your hometown, your parents, your brothers and sisters, and then you realize that you had not planned to think about them at all. Or you might suddenly discover that you are thinking about pasta and wine, or about having a lot of money to give away, or about sex, or about what you would say if Jimmy Carter gave you a phone call, or what name you would choose if they elected you Pope, or whether you could witness to Christ if you were tortured with electric shock, or about who would cry if you jumped from the fifth floor of the American College, or about how modestly you would live after you are ordained . . . and on and on. . . . You had not planned to think about these things. You had not even wanted to think about them, but you catch your mind in midstream and realize that you are moving into a complex network of ideas, images, and feelings.*

This passive, prereflective thinking is often disturbing and can make us anxious or even apprehensive. We realize that our mind thinks things that we cannot control, that sneak up on us, and that interfere with our best intentions. During the most solemn moments we may find ourselves thinking the most banal thoughts. While listening to a sermon about God's love, we find ourselves wondering about the haircut of the preacher. While reading a spiritual book, we suddenly realize that our mind is busy with the question of how much peanut butter and how much jam to put on our next sandwich. While watching a beautiful ceremony at St. Peter's, we notice ourselves trying to figure out how they will clean those thousands of surplices after the service is over. Indeed, not infrequently we catch ourselves thinking very low things during very high moments. The problem, however, is that we cannot think about nothing. We have to think, and we often feel betrayed by our own uncontrolled or uncontrollable thoughts.

Our thought processes reach even deeper than our reflective moments and our uncontrolled mental wanderings. They also reach into our sleeping hours. We might wake up in the middle of the night and find ourselves part of a frightening car race, a delicious banquet, or a heavenly choir. Sometimes we are able to give a detailed account of all the things that happened to us in our dreams: what we heard as well as what we said. Sometimes we remember only the final moment of our dream, and sometimes we are left with only a vague fear or an undefined joy. We know that much is going on during our sleep, of which, only occasionally, we catch bits and pieces. Careful brain-wave studies have shown that our mind is always active during sleep; we are always dreaming even when we have no recollection of its occurrence or its content. And, although we might tend to regard our thought processes during our night's sleep as insignificant in comparison with our reflections or our undirected mental wanderings, we should not forget that for many people dreams proved to be the main source of knowing. The patriarch Jacob heard God's call when he saw the angels going up and down a ladder; in the Old Testament Joseph was deported to Egypt because he irritated his brothers with his visions of sheaves, sun, moon, and stars bowing to him; and in the New Testament Joseph fled to Egypt after he had seen an angel warning him of Herod. And in our century, apparently so far from biblical times, we find Sigmund Freud and Carl Jung informing us that our dreams will tell us our truth.

Source of joy and sorrow

Thus we are indeed involved in unceasing thought day and night, willingly or unwillingly, during our most alert moments and during our deepest sleep, while working and while resting. This is our human predicament, a predicament that causes us great joy and immense pain. Our ceaseless thought is our burden as well as our gift. We would like to be able to stop thinking for a while. Perhaps then we would not be haunted by the memory of lost friends, by the awareness of past sins, by the knowledge of hunger and oppression in our world. These thoughts can impose themselves on us at the most unwelcome hours or keep us awake when we are most in need of sleep. So we wish that we could just be without thoughts, that we could simply erase this disturbing graffiti of our mind. But then, without thought there can be no smile, no laughter, no quiet joy. How can we be glad to see friends again when we are unable to think of them? How can we celebrate a birthday, a national holiday, or a great religious feast if our minds are not aware of the meaning of the event? How can we be grateful when we cannot remember the gifts we have received? How can we lift up our hearts and sing and dance without the thousands of thoughts that nurture our minds constantly?

Our thoughts are indeed the cradle where sorrow and joy are born. With an empty mind our hearts cannot mourn or feast, our eyes cannot cry or laugh, our hands cannot wring or clap, our tongue cannot curse or praise. Thus as "thinking reeds," we are able to feel deeply and experience life to the full with all its sorrows and joys. This unceasing thinking that lies at the core of our humanity needs to be converted slowly but persistently into unceasing prayer.

UNCEASING PRAYER

In dialogue

To pray unceasingly, as St. Paul asks us to do, would be completely impossible if it meant to think constantly about God. Not only for people who have many different concerns to occupy their minds, but also for monks who spend many hours a day in prayer, thinking about God all the time is an unrealistic desire which, if pushed too far, could lead to a mental breakdown.

To pray, I think, does not mean to think about God in contrast to thinking about other things, or to spend time with God instead of spending time with other people. Rather, it means to think and live in the presence of God. As soon as we begin to divide our thoughts into thoughts about God and thoughts about people and events, we remove God from our daily life and put him in a pious little niche where we can think pious thoughts and experience pious feelings. Although it is important and even indispensable for the spiritual life to set apart time for God and God alone, prayer can only become unceasing prayer when all our thoughts—beautiful or ugly, high or low, proud or shameful, sorrowful or joyful—can be thought in the presence of God. Thus, converting our unceasing thinking into unceasing prayer moves us from a self-centered monologue to a God-centered dialogue. This requires that we turn all our thoughts into conversation. The main question, therefore, is not so much what we think, but to whom we present our thoughts.

It is not hard to see how real a change takes place in our daily life when we find the courage to keep our thoughts to ourselves no longer, but to speak out, confess them, share them, bring them into conversation. As soon as an embarrassing or exhilarating idea is taken out of its isolation and brought into a relationship with someone, something totally new happens. This obviously requires much courage and trust, precisely because we are not always sure how our thoughts will be received. But as soon as we have taken the risk and experience acceptance, our thoughts themselves receive a new quality.

To pray unceasingly is to lead all our thoughts out of their fearful isolation into a fearless conversation with God. Jesus' life was a life lived in the presence of God his Father. Jesus kept nothing, absolutely nothing, hidden from his Father's face. Jesus' joys, his fears, his hopes, and his despairs were always shared with his Father. Therefore, Jesus could indeed say to his disciples: ". . . you will be scattered . . . leaving me alone. And yet I am not alone, because the Father is with me" (Jn. 16:32). Thus prayer asks us to break out of our monologue with ourselves and to follow Jesus by turning our lives into an unceasing conversation with our heavenly Father.

Prayer, therefore, is not introspection. Introspection means to look inward, to enter into the complex network of our mental processes in search of some inner logic or some elucidating connections. Introspection results from the desire to know ourselves better and to become more familiar with our own interiority. Although introspection has a positive role in our thought processes, the danger is that it can entangle us in the labyrinth of our own ideas, feelings, and emotions and lead us to an increasing self-preoccupation. Introspection can cause paralyzing worries or unproductive self-gratification. Introspection can also create "moodiness." This "moodiness" is a very widespread phenomenon in our society. It betrays our great concern with ourselves and undue sensitivity to how we feel or think. It makes us experience life as a constant fluctuation between "feeling high" and "feeling low," between "bad days" and "good days," and thus becomes a form of narcissism.

Prayer is not introspection. It is not a scrupulous, inward-looking analysis of our own thoughts and feelings but a careful attentiveness to him who invites us to an unceasing conversation. Prayer is the presentation of all thoughts—reflective thoughts as well as daydreams and night dreams—to our loving Father so that he can see them and respond to them with his divine compassion. Prayer is the joyful affirmation that God knows our minds and hearts and that nothing is hidden from him. It is saying with Psalm 138 (Grail translation, Paulist Press):

O Lord, you search me and you know me,
you know my resting and my rising,
you discern my purpose from afar.
You mark when I walk or lie down,
all my ways lie open to you [1–3].
O search me, God, and know my heart.
O test me and know my thoughts.
See that I follow not the wrong path
and lead me in the path of life eternal [23–24].

Prayer is a radical conversion of all our mental processes, because in prayer we move away from ourselves—our worries, preoccupations, and self-gratifications—and direct all that we recognize as ours to God in the simple trust that through his love all will be made new.

Unexpected idolatries

But this conversion from unceasing thought to unceasing prayer is far from easy. There is a deep resistance to making ourselves so vulnerable, so naked, so totally unprotected. We indeed want to love God and worship him, but we also want to keep a little corner of our inner life for ourselves, where we can hide and think our own secret thoughts, dream our own dreams, and play with our own mental fabrications. We are always tempted to select carefully the thoughts that we bring into our conversations with God.

What makes us so stingy? Maybe we wonder if God can take all that goes on in our minds and hearts. Can he accept our hateful thoughts, our cruel fantasies, and our shameful dreams? Can he handle our primitive images, our inflated illusions, and our exotic mental castles? Or do we want to hold onto our own pleasurable imaginings and stimulating reveries, afraid that in showing them to our Lord, we may have to give them up? Thus we are constantly tempted to fall back into introspection out of fear or out of greed, and to keep from our God what often is most in need of his healing touch.

This withholding from God of a large part of our thoughts leads us onto a road that we probably would never consciously want to take. It is the road of idolatry. Idolatry means the worship of false images, and that is precisely what happens when we keep our fantasies, worries, and joys to ourselves and do not present them to him who is our Lord. By refusing to share these thoughts, we limit his lordship and erect little altars to the mental images we do not want to submit to a divine conversation.

I vividly remember how I once visited a psychiatrist to complain about my difficulty in controlling my fantasy life. I told him that disturbing images kept coming up and that I found it hard to detach myself from them. When he had listened to my story, he smiled and said, "Well, Fa-

ther, as a priest you should know that this is idolatry, because your God is saying that you should not worship false images." Only then did I realize fully what it really means to confess having sinned not only in word and action but also in thought. It means confessing idolatry, one of the oldest and most pervasive temptations.

Unceasing prayer is thus extremely difficult precisely because we like to keep parts of ourselves to ourselves and experience real resistance to subjecting all that we are to God's Lordship. Unceasing prayer is indeed an ongoing struggle against idolatry. When all our thoughts—those of our days as well as those of our nights—have been brought into a loving conversation with God, then we can speak about obedience in the full sense. Since this is obviously never a task that is completed, we need to raise the question of discipline. What disciplines are there to help us in becoming disciples of Christ and living in obedience to our heavenly Father?

DISCIPLINES

Imagining Christ

Since there are so many resistances to the conversion of our unceasing thought into unceasing prayer, we need discipline. Without discipline, unceasing prayer remains a vague ideal, something that has a certain romantic appeal but that is not very realistic in our contemporary world. Discipline means that something very specific and concrete needs to be done to create the context in which a life of uninterrupted prayer can develop. Unceasing prayer requires the discipline of prayer exercises. Those who do not set aside a certain place and time each day to do nothing else but pray can never expect their unceasing thought to become unceasing prayer. Why is this planned prayer-practice so important? It is important because through this practice God can become fully present to us as a real partner in our conversation.

This discipline of prayer embraces many forms of prayer—communal as well as individual prayer, oral as well as mental prayer. It is of primary importance that we strive for prayer with the understanding that it is an explicit way of being with God. We often say, "All of life should be lived in gratitude," but this is only possible if at certain times we give thanks in a very concrete and visible way. We often say,

"All our days should be lived for the glory of God," but this is only possible if a day is regularly set apart to give glory to God. We often say, "We should love one another always," but this is only possible if we regularly perform concrete and unambiguous acts of love. Similarly, it is also true that we can only say, "All our thoughts should be prayer," if there are times in which we make God our only thought.

Common to all disciplined prayer, whether it be liturgical, devotional, or contemplative prayer, is the effort to direct all our attention to God and God alone. With this in mind, I would like to discuss in some detail the importance of the discipline of contemplation as one of the roads to unceasing prayer. Although many good things have been written about contemplation and contemplative prayer, many people still have the impression that contemplative prayer is something very special, very "high," or very difficult, and really not for ordinary people with ordinary jobs and ordinary problems. This is unfortunate because the discipline of contemplative prayer is particularly valuable for those who have so much on their minds that they suffer from fragmentation. If it is true that all Christians are called to bring their thoughts into an ongoing conversation with their Lord, then contemplative prayer can be a discipline that is especially important for those who are deeply involved in the many affairs of this world.

Contemplative prayer is prayer in which we attentively look at God. How is this possible, since nobody can see God and live? The mystery of the Incarnation is that it has become possible to see God in and through Jesus Christ. Christ is the image of God. In and through Christ, we know that God is a loving Father whom we can see by looking at his Son. When Jesus spoke to his disciples about his Father, Philip said impatiently, "Lord, let us see the Father, and then we shall be satisfied." Then Jesus answered, "To have seen me is to have seen the Father, so how can you say, 'Let us see the Father'? Do you not believe that I am in the Father and the Father is in me?" (Jn. 14:8–10). Contemplative prayer, therefore, means to see Christ as the image of God the Father. All the images consciously or unconsciously created by our minds should be made subject to him who is the only image of God. Contemplative prayer can be described as an imagining of Christ, a letting him enter fully into our consciousness so that he becomes the icon always present in our inner room. By looking at Christ with loving attention, we learn with our minds and hearts what it means that he is the way to the Father. Jesus is the only one who has seen the Father. Jesus says, "Not that anybody has seen the Father, except the one who comes from God" (Jn. 6:46). Jesus' whole being is a perpetual seeing of the Father. Jesus' life and works are an uninterrupted contemplation of his Father. For us, therefore, contemplation means an always increasing imagining of Jesus so that in, through, and with him, we can see the Father and live in his presence.

A simple example

How then do we imagine Christ such that we can indeed enter into dialogue with him and allow our unceasing thought to be transformed into unceasing prayer? There is no single answer to this question because every Christian must develop a personal discipline according to his or her task in life, work schedule, cultural heritage, and personality. It belongs to the nature of a discipline that it conforms to the needs of the individual man or woman who wants to live a life with Christ. Therefore, rather than give a general account of contemplative prayer, I will describe one example of a contemplative discipline in the hope that it might suggest different ways of prayer to different people.

One very simple discipline for contemplative prayer is to read, every evening before going to sleep, the readings of the next day's Eucharist with special attention to the Gospel. It is often helpful to take one sentence or word that offers special comfort and repeat it a few times so that, with that one sentence or word, the whole content can be brought to mind and allowed slowly to descend from the mind into the heart.

I have found this practice to be a powerful support in times of crisis. It is especially helpful during the night, when worries or anxieties may keep me awake and seduce me into idolatry. By remembering the Gospel story or any of the sayings of the Old or New Testament authors, I can create a safe mental home into which I can lead all my preoccupations and let them be transformed into quiet prayer.

During the following day, a certain time must be set apart for explicit contemplation. This is a time in which to look at Christ as he appears in the reading. The best way to do this is to read the Gospel of the day again and to imagine the Lord as he speaks or acts with his people. In this hour we can see him, hear him, touch him, and make him present to our whole being. We can see Christ as our healer, our teacher, and our guide. We can see him in his indignation, in his compassion, in his suffering, and in his glory. We can look at him, listen to him, and enter into conversation with him. Often the other readings from the Old and New Testaments help to intensify our image of Christ because, as Vincent van Gogh once said, the Gospels are the top of the mountain of which the other biblical writings form the slopes.

For me, this discipline of having an "empty time" just to be with Christ as he speaks to me in the readings of the day has proven very powerful. I have discovered that during the rest of the day, wherever I am or whatever I am doing, the image of Christ that I have contemplated during that "empty time" stays with me as a beautiful icon. Sometimes it is the conscious center of all my thoughts, but more often it is a quiet presence of which I am only indirectly aware. In the beginning I hardly noticed the difference. Slowly, however, I realized that I could carry Christ, the image of God, with me and let him affect not only my reflective thoughts but my daydreams as well. I am even convinced that this simple form of daily contemplation will eventually make my dreams again gateways of God's ongoing revelation.

Finally, this discipline puts the celebration of the Eucharist into a totally new perspective. Especially when it is celebrated in the evening, the Eucharist becomes a real climax in which the Lord with whom we have journeyed during the day speaks to us again in the context of the whole community and invites us with our friends into the intimacy of his table. It is there that the transformation of all images into the image of Christ finds its fullest realization. It is there that the unity with Christ experienced through contemplation finds its perfection. Daily contemplation makes the daily Eucharist a transforming celebration. When we live the whole day with Christ in mind and heart, the Eucharist can never be merely a routine or an obligation. Instead it becomes the center of daily life toward which everything is directed.

One of the most joyful discoveries for me was that daily contemplative prayer made me rediscover the Eucharist in its transforming power. The Eucharist became again the place from which and to which I might live; and it made me realize that even the most private form of contemplation is, in the final analysis, a service to the whole community.

This simple discipline of prayer can do much to provide a strong framework in which our unceasing thought can become unceasing prayer. In contemplative prayer, Christ cannot remain a stranger who lived long ago in a foreign world. Rather, he becomes a living presence with whom we can enter into dialogue here and now.

The contemplative practice I have described is only one of many possible examples, and I offer it merely as a suggestion that points in the direction of a disciplined prayer life. The important thing is not that we use this or that prayer technique but that we realize that the beautiful Christian ideal of making our whole life into a prayer remains nothing but an ideal unless we are willing to discipline our body, mind, and heart with a daily practice of entering directly, consciously, and explicitly into the presence of our loving Father through his Son, Jesus Christ.

CONCLUSION

I have tried to show that unceasing prayer is not just the unusual feat of a simple Russian peasant, but a realistic vocation for all Christians. It certainly is not a way of living that comes either automatically by simply desiring it or easily by just praying once in a while. But when we give it serious attention and develop an appropriate discipline, we will see a real transformation in our lives that will lead us closer and closer to God. Unceasing prayer as a permanent and unchangeable state of mind obviously will never be reached. It will always require our attention and discipline. Nevertheless, we will discover that many of the disturbing thoughts that seemed to distract us are being transformed into the ongoing praise of God. When we see with increasing clarity the beauty of the Father through his Son, we will discover that created things no longer distract us. On the contrary, they will speak in many ways about him. Then we will realize that prayer is neither more nor less than the constant practice of the presence of God at all times and in all places.

Paul's words to the Christians of Thessalonica about unceasing prayer might at first have seemed demanding and unrealistic. We can see now that they can be the source of an ever-increasing joy. After all, it is not just Paul, but also

God himself who invites us to let our whole life be transformed. That is why Paul could write: "Pray constantly and for all things give thanks to God, because this is what God expects you to do in Christ Jesus" (1 Th. 5:17).

CHAPTER IV

Contemplation and Ministry

INTRODUCTION

One name Rome certainly deserves is the city of statues. You cannot walk for long in the streets of Rome without encountering some marble character who reminds you that you are only a freshman in the school of history. Some of these characters are playful, others fierce; some beautiful, others ugly; some sensual, others spiritual. On one of these walks I met the little stone elephant with an Egyptian obelisk on his back. Looking at this cozy animal, I was reminded of a short story.

There once was a sculptor working hard with his hammer and chisel on a large block of marble. A little boy who was watching him saw nothing more than large and small pieces of stone falling away left and right. He had no idea what was happening. But when the boy returned to the studio a few weeks later, he saw to his great surprise a large, powerful lion sitting in the place where the marble had stood. With great excitement the boy ran to the sculptor and said, "Sir, tell me, how did you know there was a lion in the marble?" [Story inspired by Thomas Hora's *Existential Metapsychiatry*, (New York: Seabury Press, 1977, p. 20).]

The art of sculpture is, first of all, the art of seeing. In one block of marble, Michelangelo saw a loving mother carrying her dead son on her lap; in another, he saw a self-confident David ready to hurl his stone at the approaching Goliath; and in a third, he saw an irate Moses at the point of rising in anger from his seat. Visual art is indeed the art of seeing, and discipline is the way to make visible what has been seen. Thus the skillful artist is a liberator who frees from their bondage the figures that have been hidden for billions of years inside the marble, unable to reveal their true identity.

The image of the sculptor offers us a beautiful illustration of the relationship between contemplation and ministry. To contemplate is to *see*, and to minister is to *make visible;* the contemplative life is a life with a vision, and the life of ministry is a life in which this vision is revealed to others.

I arrived at this definition though the writings of Evagrius Ponticus, one of the Desert Fathers who had great influence on monastic spirituality in the East and the West. Evagrius calls contemplation a *theoria physike,* which means a vision (*theoria*) of the nature of things (*physike*). The contemplative is someone who sees things for what they really are, who sees the real connections, who knows—as Thomas Merton used to say—"what the scoop" is. To attain such a vision, a spiritual discipline is necessary. Evagrius calls this discipline the *praktike.* It is the taking away of the blindfolds that prevent us from seeing clearly. Merton, who was very familiar with Evagrius' thinking, expressed the same idea when he said, in a conference with the monks at the Gethsemani Abbey, that the contemplative life is a life in which we constantly move from opaqueness to transparency, from the place where things are dark, thick, impenetrable, and closed to the place where these same things are translucent, open, and offer vision far beyond themselves.

In this reflection, I would like to look first at the different levels at which this movement from opaqueness to transparency occurs in order to make it clear that all of life can become a *theoria physike*, a vision of the nature of things. Then I want to explore the *praktike*, the concrete discipline of contemplation that must undergird this movement from opaqueness to transparency if it is to remain alive. I hope that this will help us see that the relation between contemplation and ministry is as intimate as the relation between the vision and the discipline of the sculptor.

ical, Vol. II (London: Longmans, Green, and Co., 1901), p. 192.]

How differently we would live if we were constantly aware of this veil and sensed in our whole being that nature desires us to hear and see the great story of God's love to which it points. The plants and animals with whom we live teach us about birth, growth, maturation, and death, about the need for gentle care, and especially about the importance of patience and hope. And even more profoundly, water, oil, bread, and wine all point beyond themselves to the great story of our re-creation.

It is sad that in our days we no longer believe in the ministry of nature to us. We so easily limit ministry to work for people by people. But we could do an immense service to our world if we would let nature heal, counsel, and teach again. I often wonder if the sheer artificiality and ugliness with which many people are surrounded are not as bad or worse than their interpersonal problems.

I have found this painfully true in ministry to the elderly. Many old people suffer from the ugliness of their environment. Much healing could be offered to older people by helping them to make their home and room a little more beautiful. With real plants that grow and die as they do and ask for care and attention as they do, the lives of the elderly might be less lonely. There is much more going on between plants and people than we realize. Perhaps real flowers, about which and to which we can speak, have more healing power than well-chosen words about the meaning of life and death.

Those who are sensitive to the enormous ecological problem of our age and work hard to take away some of nature's opaqueness, fulfill a real ministry, because they allow not only people but also plants and animals to teach about the cycle of life, to heal the lonely, and to tell of the great love of the Lord. Thus the movement from opaqueness to transparency in our relationship with nature not only leads us to a deeper contemplation of the world that surrounds us, but also broadens our ministry of teaching, healing, and worship.

Time

A second relationship in which the contemplative life requires the ongoing movement from opaqueness to transparency is our relationship with time. Time constantly threatens to become our great enemy. In our contemporary society it often seems that not money but time enslaves us. We say, "I wish I could do all the things that I need to do, but I simply have no time. Just thinking about all the things I have to do today—writing five letters, visiting a friend, practicing my music, making a phone call, going to class, finishing a paper, doing my meditation—just thinking about these makes me tired." Indeed, it seems that many people feel they no longer have time, but that time has them. They experience themselves as victims of an ongoing pressure to meet deadlines, to be ready on time, or to make it on time. The most frequently heard excuse is, "I am sorry, but I have no time." The most common request nowadays is, "I know how busy you are, but do you have a minute?" And the most important decisions are often made over a quick lunch, or—to use an even more catching phrase—"while grabbing a bite." A strange sense of being hurried has entered into many people's lives. It seems as if the time in front of us gets filled up so quickly that we wonder, "Who or what is pushing me? It seems that I am so busy I have no time left to live."

All of this suggests that time has become opaque, dark, and impenetrable. It is time experienced as *chronos*. Life is nothing more than a chronology, a randomly collected series of incidents and accidents over which we have no control. To experience life in this way can soon lead us to a sense of fatalism. This fatalism often manifests itself under the guise of boredom. Boredom does not mean that we have nothing to do or that there is not enough going on to entertain us, but that we are gnawed by the feeling that whatever we do or say makes no real difference. It is the feeling that the real decisions are made independent of our words or actions.

Boredom, therefore, is a symptom of living in time as *chronos*. The paradox of *chronos* is that precisely when we are in a hurry, overly busy, or rushing to meet deadlines, we are most subject to boredom. This reveals how opaque time has become for us.

The contemplative life is a life in which time slowly loses its opaqueness and becomes transparent. This is often a very difficult and slow process, but it is full of re-creating power. To start seeing that the many events of our day, week, or year are not in the way of our search for a full life, but rather the way to it, is a real experience of conversion. If we start discovering that writing letters, attending classes, visiting people, and cooking food are not a series of random events that prevent us from realizing our deepest self, but contain within themselves the transforming power we are looking for, then we are beginning to move from time lived as *chronos* to time lived as *kairos. Kairos* means *the* opportunity. It is the right time, the real moment, the chance of our life. When our time becomes *kairos*, it opens up endless new possibilities and offers us a constant opportunity for a change of heart.

In Jesus' life every event becomes *kairos*. He opens his public ministry with the words, "The time has come" (Mk. 1:15), and he lives every moment of it as an opportunity. Finally, he announces that his time is near (Mk. 26:10) and enters into his last hour as *the kairos*. In so doing he liberates history from its fatalistic chronology.

This really is good news because now we know that all the events of life, even such dark events as war, famine and flood, violence and murder, are not irreversible fatalities but rather carry within themselves the possibility of becoming *the* moment of change. Then what seemed nothing more than flying pieces of marble begins to reveal itself as the necessary and painful removal of what prevented us from seeing the true image of God. Then we no longer need to run from the present in search of the place where we think life is really happening. We can see in the center of the present the first manifestation of the Kingdom. Then boredom can no longer exist, because every moment is filled with infinite meaning. Then, indeed, time becomes transparent.

The contemplative life, therefore, is not a life that offers a few good moments between the many bad ones, but a life that transforms all our time into a window through which the invisible world becomes visible.

It belongs to the core of all ministry to make time transparent so that in the most concrete circumstances of life we can see that our hour is God's hour and that all time is therefore *kairos*. All who suffer—especially the elderly, the poor, and those who are physically, mentally, or spiritually imprisoned—are tempted by fatalism. When we can break the chains of this fatalism and help others to see the real nature of what takes place in their lives, then we really are bringing good news to the poor, new sight to the blind, and liberty to the captives (Lk. 4:18).

People

The third relationship that invites the contemplative to move from opaqueness to transparency is our relationship with people. Here more than in the two previous relationships, the importance of contemplation as *theoria physike*—as seeing the real connections—becomes manifest. One of our greatest temptations is to relate to people as interesting characters, as individuals who strike us as worthy of special attention because of their special qualities. We are always intrigued by interesting characters, whether they are film stars or criminals, sports heroes or killers, Nobel Prize winners or perverts. Sometimes, our attention is instinctively drawn to these unusual individuals. We want to meet them, shake their hands, get their autograph, or just gaze at them. Magazines such as *People* make millions of dollars catering to human curiosity about humans, and the front pages of most newspapers give less and less news and more and more reports about new records in human irregularities, whether they lead to praise or to blame.

Rome is probably one of the best cities in which to observe this—remarkably enough, on both sides of the Tiber. Not only do newspapers like Il Messaggero *and* Il Corriere della Sera *create the illusion that the land is dominated by kidnapers and the sky by hijackers, but also the clerical world proves to be richly endowed with curious characters.*

As long as people are little more than interesting characters to us, they remain opaque. We can be quite sure that no one who is approached as an interesting character is going to reveal to us his or her secret. On the contrary, characterization is often so narrowing and limiting that it makes people close themselves and hide. Especially in the field of the helping professions, the temptation to label people with easy characterizations is great, since it gives us the illusion of understanding. Not only psychiatric labels such as "neurotic," "psychopathic," or "schizophrenic," but also religious labels such as "unbeliever," "pagan," "sinner," "progressive," "conservative," "liberal," and "orthodox" can give us a false sense of understanding that reveals more about our insecurities than about the real nature of our neighbors.

Our great task is to prevent our fears from boxing our fellow human beings into characterizations and to see them as persons. The word "person" comes from *per-sonare,* which means "sounding through." Our vocation in life is to be and increasingly become persons who "sound through" to each other a greater reality than we ourselves fully know. As persons we sound through a love greater than we ourselves can grasp, a truth deeper than we ourselves can articulate, and a beauty richer than we ourselves can contain. As persons we are called to be transparent to each other, to point far beyond our character to him who has given us his love, truth, and beauty.

When someone says to you, "I love you," or "I am deeply moved by you," or "I am grateful to you," you easily become defensive and wonder what is so special about you. You say or think "Aren't there many other people who are

much more lovable or much more intelligent than I am?"
But then you have forgotten that you are a person who
sounds through to others something much greater and
deeper than you yourself can hear.

Contemplation as *theoria physike,* as seeing what is really
there, has a very significant meaning in the context of interpersonal relationships. Although we cannot hear ourselves
sounding through, we are nevertheless sounding through to
each other. This implies that our real gifts only become
known to us when they are recognized and affirmed by
those who receive them.

Here we can begin to see the intimate connection between contemplation and ministry. Contemplation enables
us to see the gifts in those to whom we minister, and ministry is first of all the reception and affirmation of what we
hear sounding through them so that they themselves may
come to a recognition of their own giftedness. What more
beautiful ministry is there than the ministry through which
we help others to become aware of the love, truth, and
beauty they reveal to us? Ours is a time in which many
people doubt their self-worth and are often on the verge of a
self-condemnation that can lead to suicide. We can indeed
save lives by discovering in those in need the gifts that ask
to be shared.

Innumerable people suffer from being unable to give anything. Young people often feel that they know little or nothing; adults often doubt that they have a real contribution to

make; and millions of people in the cities, towns, and villages of this world wonder if they are of any importance to anyone. How beautiful, then, is the ministry through which we call forth the hidden gifts of people and celebrate with them the love, truth, and beauty they give us. Ministry and contemplation therefore enrich each other and lead to an always increasing joy, for God continues to reveal himself to us in the ever changing lives of people.

So we see how contemplation requires a constant movement from opaqueness to transparency. It is the movement from nature as a property to be possessed to nature as a gift to be received with admiration and gratitude. It is the movement from time as a randomly thrown-together series of incidents and accidents to time as a constant opportunity for a change of heart. Finally, it is the movement from people as interesting characters to people as persons sounding through more than they themselves can contain. This does not mean that nature is never property, that time is never *chronos*, and that people are never interesting characters. It *does* mean that if these were to become the dominant modes of relating to our world, our world would remain opaque and we would never see how things really hang together. When, however, we are able slowly to remove our blindfolds and see nature as gift, time as *kairos*, and people as persons, we will also see that our whole world is a sacrament that constantly reveals to us the great love of God. That is the *theoria physike* about which Evagrius spoke.

CONTEMPLATIVE PRAYER

The lion in the heart

We now have to speak about the practice of contemplative prayer. If we look at the *theoria physike* without also looking at the *praktike*, we can easily develop a romantic view of contemplation and its relationship to ministry. Contemplation is indeed a way of living in which all of creation —nature, time, and people—becomes transparent and speaks to us about God and his love for us. But this all-embracing view of contemplation might suggest that ministry and contemplation are simply the same. This, however, would be an oversimplification. If we say, "My work is my prayer," we forget that the act of seeing requires a well-trained eye.

The little boy's question to the sculptor is a very real question, perhaps the most important question of all: "Sir, tell me, how did you know that there was a lion in the marble?" How do we know that God can become visible through the veil of nature? How do we come to the realization that all of our time can become an occasion for a change of heart? How do we know that people sound through more than they themselves can hear? It is certainly not obvious. For most people, the world is very opaque. They see nothing in the marble but a thick, impenetrable block of stone. Aren't we romantics, after all, people who are unwilling to see the hard facts of life and who simply see what we want to see?

We touch here the central question of our spiritual life and our ministry. Is there a lion in the marble? Is there a God in this world? Or is our spiritual life nothing more than wishful thinking and our ministry nothing other than the creation of a collective illusion in which everyone sees God but no one sees the bitter reality of our daily existence? Do we see a lion in the marble and yet not see that it really blocks our way?

There *is* an answer to the boy's question, an answer that irritates many and makes sense to only a few. The answer is, "I knew there was a lion in the marble because before I saw the lion in the marble I saw him in my own heart. The secret is that it was the lion in my heart who recognized the lion in the marble."

The practice of contemplative prayer is the discipline by which we begin to see God in our heart. It is a careful attentiveness to him who dwells in the center of our being such that through the recognition of his presence we allow him to take possession of all our senses. Through the discipline of prayer we awaken ourselves to the God in us and let him enter into our heartbeat and our breathing, into our thoughts and emotions, our hearing, seeing, touching, and tasting. It is by being awake to this God in us that we can see him in the world around us. The great mystery of the contemplative life is not that we see God in the world, but that God within us recognizes God in the world. God speaks to God, Spirit speaks to Spirit, heart speaks to heart. Contemplation, therefore, is a participation in this divine self recognition. It is the divine Spirit praying in us who makes our world transparent and opens our eyes to the presence of the divine Spirit in all that surrounds us. It is with our heart of hearts that we see the heart of the world. This explains the intimate relationship between contemplation and ministry.

> *St. Francis spoke with the sun, the moon, and the animals not because he was a naïve romantic, but because his ascetic discipline had awakened him to the God of his heart and so enabled him to see the Lord in all that surrounded him. The Little Brothers and Sisters of Jesus enjoy inconspicuous and often monotonous work not because they do not see the real condition in which they work, but because they recognize in the midst of the human struggle the God whose loving care they saw in their hour of adoration. The Missionaries of Charity experience God's presence amid the poorest of the poor because they experienced his presence in the intimacy of their contemplation. And thus all real ministry finds its source in a well-trained heart where God's presence has been made known.*

To know God in the world requires knowing him by heart. To know God by heart is the purpose of a contemplative discipline. It is a very hard discipline, especially for those of us who are "heady" people. But if we are serious about the task of ministry, we must be willing to engage in the tough and often agonizing struggle to break through all our mental defenses and know our God by heart.

Simple and obedient

Let us not underestimate the intensity of this struggle. Surrounded by books, papers, and professors, and inundated by lectures, talks, presentations, chats, and chitchat, we are constantly in danger of letting God's Word become caught in the network of our clever distinctions, elaborate arguments, and sheer verbosity. As ministers of the Word of God, we urgently need a discipline of contemplative prayer. The two main characteristics of contemplative prayer that seem to be particularly important here are simplicity and obedience.

Our contemplation should first of all be simple, very simple. Contemplative prayer enables us to allow the Word of God to descend from our mind into our heart, where it can become fruitful. That is why it is so important to avoid all long inner reasoning and inner speeches and to focus quietly on a word or sentence. Then we must ruminate on it, murmur it, chew it, eat it, so that in our innermost self we can really sense its power.

Second, our prayer should be obedient. The word "obedience" comes from the word *audire*, which means to listen.

Contemplative prayer requires that we listen, that we let God speak to us when he wants and in the way he wants. This is difficult for us precisely because it means allowing God to say what we might not want to hear. But if we listen long and deeply, God will reveal himself to us as a soft breeze or a still, small voice; he will offer himself to us in gentle compassion. Without this obedience, this listening to the God of our heart, we will remain deaf and our life will grow absurd. The word "absurd" includes the term *surdus*, which means deaf. The absurd life is the opposite of the obedient life.

Thus simple and obedient contemplative prayer is the way we come to know God by heart. When we know him by heart, then we will also recognize him in our world, its nature, its history, and its people.

The discipline of contemplative prayer is the basis of the contemplative life. Now we may understand more clearly that this same discipline also undergirds all ministry.

CONCLUSION

In these reflections I have tried to give a contemporary meaning to the *theoria physike*, the vision of the nature of things, and the *praktike*, the discipline of prayer. I have called the *theoria physike* the contemplative life and the *praktike* contemplative prayer. In this conclusion I would like to point out that, according to Evagrius, *praktike* and *theoria physike* find their culmination in *theologia*. This *theologia* is the direct knowledge of God that leads to the contemplation of the Holy Trinity. Here we go beyond the practice of contemplative prayer, and even beyond the vision of the nature of things, and enter into a most intimate communion with God himself. This *theologia* is the greatest gift of all, the grace of complete unity, rest, and peace. It is the highest level of spiritual life, in which the created world is transcended and we experience directly our being lifted up into God's inner life. In this experience, the distinction between ministry and contemplation is no longer necessary, since here there are no more blindfolds to remove and all has become seeing.

This *theologia* is the Mount Tabor experience in our lives. It is an experience that is given only to a few, and even they must return to the valley, while being told not to tell others what they have seen. For most of us, the greater part of our life is spent not on the mountaintop but in the valley. And in this valley we are called to be contemplative ministers.

I began with the story of the boy and the sculptor. It was meant as a parable that might help you see the intimate connection between ministry and contemplation. I conclude with the hope that we will find not only the courage to remove blindfolds and reveal God's presence in this valley of tears but also the joy of recognizing God's grace when someone asks us with excitement, "Sir, tell me, how did you know there was a lion in the marble?" Every time that question is raised, we know once more where our ministry begins.

Postscript

White on our faces

The four chapters of this book were written as a response to some very concrete questions of English-speaking men and women living in Rome. When, however, I look back on these reflections and try to see them as a whole, it seems that their value might go beyond those who raised the questions. I wonder if every human being has not known in some way and at some time the desire for solitude, for inner vacancy, for prayer, and for contemplation. Don't all men and women experience the urge to be alone with God, to create space for him in the center of their lives, to lift up all the needs of the world to him, and to see more clearly where he reveals himself to us? Mostly these desires and urges remain hidden or are quickly washed away by the waves of our engagements and involvements, but they never seem to vanish completely. Especially during the last decades many people have become more aware of their "other side" and have expressed the hope of finding guidance in bringing this side more into the foreground of their consciousness.

Solitude, celibacy, prayer, and contemplation are values for all people, but some men and women have the unique vocation to give special visibility to these values and to guard them with special care. Whenever these values are lived out authentically and generously, what becomes visible is not a spiritual virtuosity good for a select few, but a way of life which speaks to many.

Between the frightening acts of the heroes of this world, there is a constant need for clowns, people who by their empty, solitary lives of prayer and contemplation reveal to us our "other side" and thus offer consolation, comfort, hope, and a smile. Rome is a good city in which to become aware of the need for clowns. This large, busy, entertaining, and distracting city keeps tempting us to join the lion tamers and trapeze artists who get most of the attention. But whenever the clowns appear we are reminded that what really counts is something other than the spectacular and the sensational. It is what happens between the scenes. The clowns show us by their "useless" behavior, not simply that many of our preoccupations, worries, tensions, and anxieties need a smile, but more important that we, too, have white on our faces and that we, too, are called to clown a little.

I have discovered some very beautiful clowns in Rome, holy men and women whose tears always hide a smile and whose smiles always hide a tear. They have encouraged me not to wipe off the white on my face but to add some to it. I hope that you who have read this book will also feel encouraged to use more clown white and experience in your own lives the preciousness of solitude, celibacy, prayer, and contemplation.